The science behind canine raw feeding

by H B Turner

To my furry babies, my inspiration and joy. I will always love you.

About the Author

In 1999, on return from a business trip to America, H B Turner (Hope) bought a raw fed kitten. Other than the bones she remembered getting from the butcher for her beloved Chow Chow as a child, this was her first introduction to raw feeding.

In 2002, Hope found a dog she fell in love with and started researching further, as the dog was raw fed. In early 2003, she then bought two raw fed puppies and the research began in earnest, including taking a number of short courses.

Having believed that she had exhausted the non-academic route, in 2009 Hope returned to full time education, taking first a Foundation Degree in Animal Management and Welfare, and then 'toping up' to a Bachelors degree in Applied Animal Studies in 2012. Throughout her studies each assignment was tailored as much as possible to scientific research on the differentials between raw and conventional feeding and its benefits.

During this time, Hope chose to use social media as a platform to teach what she had learnt and created a number of recipes which she believed were healthier than many of the market alternatives.

Hope is currently lecturing at seminars on raw feeding, taking her Master's degree, and hoping to launch a Canine Nutrition Clinic in the near future.

For details of how to get hold of her, go to her website at:

www.Healthful.uk.com

Contents

About the Author.. 4

Introduction... 7

History of canine domestication 9

History of dog food 13

Canine digestion... 17

Pet food Industry 23

Ingredients.. 25

Ingredient effects on digestion 31

Effects of cooking 32

Scientific Research 37

    Case Study – Dawson 41

What should your dog eat?................................ 43

Recipes 49

Herbs and Spices... 67

FAQ's 71

References 83

Useful Links:... 92

Introduction

Today's "Nescafe society" encourages us to rely on information provided by experts in their field - which is a totally logical and time saving attitude to have. Unfortunately, this can open the floodgates to those who would profit from our naivety.

In January of 2009, the British Government started its "Change 4 Life" campaign, in which it advised people to live a healthier lifestyle, thus taking the strain off the National Health Service, a great deal of which is due to Obesity, non-genetic Diabetes and Heart Disease.

There is a plethora of literature available to us with regard to diet, for slimming purposes and/or for health. These fly off the shelves at a rate of knots whilst we struggle to balance work and home life, and also attempt to emulate the ones who appear healthier and fitter than the rest of us: our genetically programmed ideal (survival of the fittest).

Whilst many of us make time to research what we can do to improve our own health, very few think it necessary or have the time to do the same for their pets. Most people trust the experts, the pet food manufacturers and veterinarians, whom they pay to keep their beloved pet healthy.

It has become socially understood that eating "organic" fresh fruit, vegetables, and meat is much healthier for us than the chemically treated and preserved alternatives. However, this logic does not seem to have spread to our animals, where convenience is the word of the day.

There are many types of diet available for our pets and the majority of owners use pre-packaged dried or wet food: it is convenient and we are advised by advertising and veterinary practitioners that it is a complete diet, nutritious, healthy and will fill our animal with vitality.

Within the dried and wet food varieties there are a great number of options: different manufacturers, variations for all ages of pet, claims of being healthier than competitors etc., etc.

With convenience being a norm in today's society, with microwavable meals, fast food and takeaways being a staple in our busy lives, those who are even aware of the option of feeding other than pre-packaged are either too busy to properly consider it, or think it would be too complicated or difficult to implement, or commit to it totally, generally for life.

In the world of raw feeding dog owners, the sentence "That dog eats better than I do!" is heard more often than you would think - and most of the time never a truer word were spoke!. In today's world of fast foods, GM crops and toxic pollution, it is becoming increasingly difficult to eat a healthy diet, unless you can afford organic and have the time to prepare most of your own meals from scratch. The same can generally be said for our pets.

History of canine domestication

A domestic animal is defined as "one that has been bred in captivity for purposes of economic profit to a human community that maintains total control over its breeding, organization of territory and food supply". (Clutton-Brock, 1999).

The evolution of living organisms, the physical adaptation to environment over generations, or "mutability of species" (Darwin, 1859) is a result of 'Natural Selection', where "healthy and vigorous individuals have better chances of surviving and leaving progeny" (Dobzhansky *et al.* 1977).

Earth is home to a vast array of different Species and sub-species, which are a result of 'Speciation' (species specialisation leading to adaptation and therefore new species and sub-species). Speciation occurs in two forms: either by physical separation and sub-populations adapting to their local habitat (Coyne & Orr, 2004), or when a species is located in the same area, but divides into groups who specialise in different ways and then begin to adapt to their chosen specialisation, i.e. some may specialise in hunting different types of prey and adapt accordingly.

However, domestication is due to the artificial selection of man.

There is archaeological evidence to suggest that wolves, unchanged physically for over 1,000,000 years (wolfcountry.net, N.D.), were domesticated between 15,000 and 40,000 years ago. The oldest evidence for a working relationship between man and dog, is at the Bonn-Oberkassel site, 14,000 years ago (Morey, 2006). However, mitochondrial DNA analysis suggests that this relationship goes back between 40 and 135 thousand years (Ostrander & Wayne, 2005). Human selective breeding from these ancient canids has led to the domestic dogs of today. This evolutionary theory (Figure 1) is further backed by DNA proof that domestic dogs are descended from wolves (Burns, 2009), even if the molecular distance is more than 100,000 BP, well before the advent of canine domestication (Clutton-Brock, 1999). The domestic dog, can be traced back to three female wolves from East Asia (Townend, 2009), although it is likely that current dog breeds have evolved from difference types of wolf (Clutton-Brock, 1999), further backed by iconography through the ages showing distinct types of dog in certain areas (Riddle, 1987).

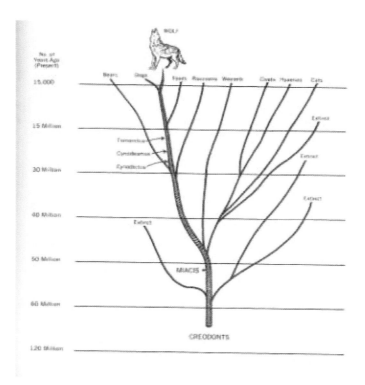

Figure 1 (Mech, 1981)

10

Subsequent evidence of domestication dates back to around 7000BC, within 3000 years of the end of the previous Ice Age.

One theory of the beginning of domestication is that, due to man's behaviour of creating a camp, clearing land around it, and throwing rubbish outside of camp boundaries (Budiansky, 1992), animals found that humans provided easily accessible food. The settling of man and consequential enlargement of these camps would have provided reliable food for the wild animals, thus reducing the animals' fear and slowly building up a relationship between wild animals and man. This leads to the theory that wild animals domesticated themselves.

Research with Siberian Silver Foxes by Dr. Dmitri Belyaev in 1959, led to the discovery that a predisposition to domestication/tameness is genetic, and can be selectively bred (Cornell University, N.D.). His research showed that the tameness could be bred in within six generations. However, this domestic fox had floppy ears, demonstrating neotony (the retention of juvenile features in the adult animal), and shorter legs than its ancestor (Townend, 2009). It is therefore logical to assume that something similar occurred in early domestication.

Canine evolution specialised through tandem repeats of DNA (Savolainen *et al.* 2000) (an exaggeration of a particular attribute) via selective breeding, which has shaped the dog breeds we have today. They have only been separated into breeds, however, for around 300-400 years, and we have only had a central register for breeds in the UK since 1873 (The Kennel Club).

Each animal has an 'instinctive flight distance' a range at which it will allow a predator to approach before it attempts escape (Budiansky, 1992). This is followed by a 'run distance', an innate distance an animal will run from its pursuer (Roberts, 1996). This implies that the first people to keep wild animals as pets, were either proficient at communication with the animals to such an extent as to draw them in willingly, or organised enough to herd them into a corral/captive area and prevent their escape. In all probability, both of these theories are correct.

Domestication would have meant a life protected from the daily threat of predators and hunger for the animals, as well as a useful extra hunting tool and/or flock protection for humans, thus increasing the life expectancy, and reducing the energy expenditure of both. Of course, after thousands of years of selective breeding, many domestic species of plant and animal would now not be able to survive in the wild (Skelton, 1993). For example, Chihuahuas often require a caesarean section in order to reproduce.

After domestication, habituation to humans leading to increased tameness would have been seen to increase through the generations, most likely due to selective breeding and experimentation (as in Belyaev's experiment, detailed above). This selective breeding and experimentation, though presumably initially to increase ease of handling, would have progressed to experimentation for an increase in productivity, hence the differing breed types we have today i.e. Working, Gundog, Hound, Pastoral, Terrier, Toy, Utility.

History of dog food

"The wolfs' diet consists almost entirely of highly concentrated and easily digested fat and protein", obtained by the majority from deer, moose, caribou, elk, sheep, beaver, bison and hare. Their preference when it comes to domestic animals i.e. the food stuffs that dog owners can easily obtain are: cattle, sheep, deer, horse, pig and goat (Mech, 1970). Smaller prey are known to be mice, mink, muskrats, squirrels, rabbits, birds, fish, lizards & snakes in addition to grass-hoppers, earthworms, berries and duck.

Wolves tend to eat in a specific order, first rump, then intestines, followed by heart, lungs, and liver, but never the stomach (Mech, 1970).

Wolves assisting the hunt were undoubtedly fed scraps from the kill and are known to have scavenged waste from human encampments (Serpell, 1995). The delineation between working dogs and pets cannot have occurred until there was inequality within the realms of men, as basic hunter-gatherers would not have had a food surplus for non-productive pets.

The first dog-specific food was a biscuit sold in 1856 by James Spratt (Purina, N.D.). This biscuit was made from wheat, vegetables, beetroot and beef blood (see figure 2), very similar to the Bonio made today by Nestlé.

CAUTION.—It is most essential that when purchasing you see that every Cake is stamped **SPRATT'S PATENT**, or unprincipled dealers, for the sake of a trifle more profit, which the makers allow them, may serve you with a spurious and highly dangerous imitation.

SPRATT'S PATENT
MEAT FIBRINE DOG CAKES.

From the reputation these Meat Fibrine Cakes have now gained, they require scarcely any explanation to recommend them to the use of every one who keeps a dog ; suffice it to say they are free from salt, and contain "dates," the exclusive use of which, in combination with meat and meal to compose a biscuit, is secured to us by Letters Patent, and without which no biscuit so composed can possibly be a successful food for dogs.

Price 22s. per cwt., carriage paid; larger quantities, 20s. per cwt., carriage paid.

" Royal Kennels, Sandringham, Dec. 20th, 1873.

" To the Manager of Spratt's Patent.

"Dear Sir,—In reply to your enquiry, I beg to say I have used your biscuits for the last two years, and never had the dogs in better health. I consider them invaluable for feeding dogs, as they insure the food being perfectly cooked, which is of great importance   "Yours faithfully,   C. H. JACKSON."

" 36, North Great George Street, Dublin, June 9th, 1874.

"Gentlemen,—Please to forward to my private residence, as above, 4 cwt. of Dog Biscuits as before ; let them be precisely the same as those supplied on all former occasions   I have much pleasure in bearing personal testimony to their suitability and general efficiency for greyhounds, and in adding that my greyhound, Royal Mary, winner at Altcar of last year's Waterloo Plate, was almost entirely trained for all her last year's engagements upon them.   "Yours obediently,   WILLIAM J. DUNBAR, M.A."

" Rhiwlas, Bala, 21st June, 1873.

" Sir,—I have now tried your Dog Cakes for some six months or so in my kennels, and am happy to be able to give a conscientious testimonial in their favour.   I have also found them valuable for feeding horses on a long journey, when strength and stamina are important objects.   It was the opinion of my brother judges and myself that dogs never appeared at the close of a week's confinement in better health and condition than the specimens exhibited at the Crystal Palace Show, and I understand that your Cakes are exclusively used by the manager.   "R. J. LLOYD PRICE."

Figure 2 - Advert for Spratts from 1876   (British Veterinary Journal, 1876)

In the 1920's canned dog food was introduced by Chappel Bros Inc. under the name Ken-L-Ration (see figure 3). This was mostly horse meat, as in the 1930's vast numbers of horses and mules, confiscated for the war effort, were no longer required and being replaced by cars and tractors after World War I.

Figure 3 - Advertisement for Ken-L-Ration (Ken-L-Ration, 1932).

Once the war supply had run out a lack of horse meat and concerns over the costs of feeding fresh meat and vegetables, led to the use of waste products from the human food industry and the initiation of dried foods. Changing from the use of expensive ingredients to grains for energy, legumes for calcium, seeds for fat soluble vitamins etc. (McNamara, 2006).

Dried food as it is known today started hitting the shelves in large bags made by Purina in 1957. The popularity of dried food increased dramatically in the 1980's and has seen an increase in market share of 90% in the last decade (PFMA, 2011).

Canine digestion

Dogs have strong stomach acid and a relatively short intestinal tract, with a fast transit time (Mash, 2011). An incorrect diet can produce changes in absorptive function, which are associated with damage to colonic microstructure (Rolfe et al., 2002).

Apprehension

Canine teeth and the scissor action of their jaw have evolved to puncture and rip flesh from carcasses, with shearing carnassials (Wayne & Vila, 2001) and crushing post-carnassials (Bradshaw, 2006) (see Figure 4).

Figure 4 – Canine Head

Mastication & Swallowing

Dogs have little to no lateral jaw movement due to the grounding of the temperomandibular joint by the post-glenoid process, preventing the possibility of dislocation during the hunt (Mech & Boitani, 2003), no flattened teeth (Goody, 1997) and are not designed to chew fibrous plant matter.

The salivary glands of a dog (Parotid, Mandibular, Sublingual, Buccal and Zygomatic) do not produce amylase (Altman & Dittmer, 1968), necessary for digesting starch, as starch is not a large part of their natural daily intake.

Dogs have a wide oesophagus to allow large pieces of torn-off food to pass to the stomach, due to the limited amount of mastication performed.

Stomach

The canine stomach is where the majority of food breakdown occurs through a combination of churning and gastric juices.

Gastrin is released from the stomach wall, which activates the release of hydrochloric acid at a pH of 1-2 (National Research Council, 2006). This pH level is kept high by protein, but reduced by grains, rendering lipase irreversibly inactive below pH 1.5 and negatively effecting pepsin activity over pH 2.0, (Carriere *et al.*, 1991: Maskell & Johnson, 1993). In laymen's terms this means that a high meat protein content has a positive effect on digestion however, grains can have a negative effect.

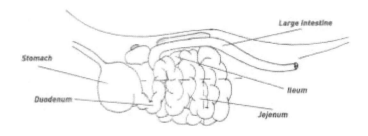

Figure 5 – The Digestive Tract (Griffith, 2012)

Duodenum

Chime passes from the stomach to the duodenum after 4-8 hours. Pancreatic enzymes and bile continue the breakdown of food. When working at peak efficiency pancreatic enzymes and bile at a pH of 7.1-8.2 (Banta *et al.,* 1979) are bacteriocidal (kill) for Escherichia Coli, Shigella, Salmonella and Klebsiella and bacteriostatic (render unable to reproduce) for coagulase positive and negative Staphylococci and Pseudomonas, whilst inhibiting Candida Albicans (National Research Council, 2006). However, bile release is in response to lipids (fats), but only to the right lipids (Erasmus,

19

1993).Therefore, low fat diets will have reduced bile release and thus an increased risk of contraction of said pathogens.

Jejunum

The jejunum is lined with villi, further capturing nutrients. Proteins enable beneficial flora "good bacteria" (i.e. Lactobacillus acidophilus, Bifidobacterium bifidum etc.) to flourish in this environment, however refined sugar and starch molecules change the environment, making it unsuitable for the 'good' bacteria to breed and feeding the "bad bacteria" and fungi (i.e. Salmonella, Clostridium, Candida etc.). This can create an imbalance in this rather large part of the immune system.

Ileum

Short chain fatty acids derived from unabsorbed starch and fibre stimulate motility of the ileum (Scheppach, 1994: Kamath *et al.,* 1987) inhabited by anaerobic bacteria (National Research Council, 2006). i.e. larger quantities of starch than the dog can naturally digest, due to the small quantity of amylase (starch digesting enzyme) created and released from the pancreas, speed up movement through the ileum, reducing its ability to absorb nutrients.

Large Intestine

Movement is vital to the large intestine via peristalsis. Certain foods can affect the speed of movement and cause constipation. This movement is slowed down if the diet is not meat based (Clemens and Stevens, 1980), but can be sped up by high fibre content, possibly leading to reduced absorption of electrolytes and water (National Research Council, 2006).

Anus

Anal Glands are naturally expressed if the faecal matter passed is firm (Ashdown, 2008: Gordon, 2001).

Pet food Industry

Commercial cooked diets have differing processes.

Dry food, which contains raw and pre-cooked ingredients, is mixed, heat and pressure extruded, formed, dried into shape and then coated (Pet Food Institute, 2010).

(Basically, let's for hypothetical reasons take your Sunday Roast Dinner: cook it until it becomes dust, add water to shape it, re-bake it and then spray it with oil.)

Canned or tinned food also contains both raw and pre-cooked ingredients, which are heat cooked and sterilised (Pedigree Pet Foods, 1993).

A raw diet, on the other hand, is either served fresh or frozen to maintain shelf life. Fatty Acids are not broken down by freezing, even up to -80°, however, most cells and whole organisms are (Pond, 2000). In effect, the freezing process can destroy most pathogenic bacteria in the same way as cooking, but without the deleterious effect of destroying the nutrients required for the health and wellbeing of the consumer.

Regardless of nutritional differences between raw and cooked diet ingredients, the digestibility of those nutrients in the form it is provided in is affected. The cooking process affects vitamin retention, the nature of proteins, digestibility and cellular use of the resultant food stuffs.

Nutritional recommendations

The Waltham Centre for Pet Nutrition has produced a list of minimum nutrient requirements for dogs per 400 Kilocalories (Kcal) of metabolisable energy (Kelly & Wills, 1996). However, this list only details, 5 of the 7 major minerals, (generally required in large amounts by all animals), 6 of 10 essential trace minerals, 12 vitamins, fat and protein content and 1 fatty acid. There are no recommendations for the myriad of other vitamins, minerals and amino acids currently accepted by the BSAVA (British Small Animal Veterinary Association), nor is there such a thing as a Recommended Daily Allowance (RDA) as with human guidelines, or any estimate of safe levels of nutritional bioavailability (Burger & Rivers, 1989).

Ingredients

UK made cooked pet foods may contain the following ingredients:

- "material from animals that passed inspection for human consumption prior to slaughter - hides, skins, horns, feet, pig bristle, feather and blood (unless they are from ruminants requiring TSE testing, in which case they can only be used if they are tested and give a negative result)

- material from on farm slaughter of rabbits and poultry

- hatchery waste, eggs, egg by-products and day old chicks killed for commercial reasons

- fish and by-products from fish processing plants

- material from the production of food including degreased bones
- products of animal origin (POA) or foodstuffs containing products of animal origin no longer intended for human consumption for commercial reasons or because of packaging problems, etc.

- PAP derived from the above materials • imported pet food

- pet food and feeding stuffs of animal origin, or feeding stuffs containing animal by-products or derived products, which are no longer intended for feeding for commercial reasons or due to problems of manufacturing or packaging defects or other defects from which no risk to public or animal health arises,

- blood, placenta, wool, feathers, hair, horns, hoof cuts and raw milk originating from live animals that did not show any signs of disease communicable through that product to humans or animals

- aquatic animals, and parts of such animals, except sea mammals, which did not show any signs of disease communicable to humans or animals

- animal by-products from aquatic animals originating from establishments or plants manufacturing products for human consumption.

- shells from shellfish with soft tissue or flesh

- hatchery by-products

- eggs and egg by-products

- day old chicks killed for commercial reasons

- some species of aquatic and terrestrial invertebrates

- some rodents and lagomorphs (rabbits)."

UK made raw pet food may contain:

- "Only material from slaughterhouses, or game killed for human consumption, can be used in raw pet food manufacture. (EU Control Regulation Article 10 (a) and (b) (i) and (ii)). Material that:

- has been passed as fit for human consumption but is not going to be used in this way for commercial reasons. e.g. clean tripe

- came from animals that passed ante-mortem inspection but was rejected as unfit for human consumption, e.g. livers with fluke. For such material to be used there must not have been any signs of communicable disease. " (Defra, 2011)

Therefore there is legally a significant difference in what can be included in these cooked and raw products.

Basically the pet food you are buying be it wet or dry is made up of Industrial Waste, this includes:-

- The rancid oil from the food industry
- Burnt chocolate unfit for human consumption (Chocolate is poisonous to dogs)
- Feathers which increase the protein levels but are indigestible
- Anti-oxidants have to be added to the mix because of the fact that this food is rancid
- extra vitamins and minerals are added, but before cooking at between 220 and 270 degrees F for between 20 and 60 minutes, which of course breaks down most of the vitamins and minerals that were still present
- Large skips are filled with meat left over from the docks or our supermarkets, this goes into our pets food still in its' polystyrene containers, along with the fag butts and coffee cups of the people filling the containers.

I quote: "Vegetable waste, bakery and biscuit waste etc. that comes from premises that handle meat may now be fed to livestock."

Other ingredients

There are of course other ingredients than meat and meat derivatives in commercially available pet food. These are mostly grains:-

- Corn :
  - Corn Flour
  - Corn Bran
  - Corn Gluten meal

- Wheat :
  - Wheat Flour – including sweepings
  - Wheat germ meal –
  - Wheat middlings and shorts – including sweepings

- Beet Pulp – added for fibre, primarily sugar.
- Soybean meal
- Powdered cellulose – a bulking agent
- Sugar foods by-products – the inedible by-products of the sugar and sweet industry
- Shells – ground almond and peanut shells for fibre

but also include, but are not restricted to :-

- Preservatives:

BHA and BHT, both suspected to be carcinogens, research shows that they also can initiate birth defects and damage to liver and kidneys.

Ethoxyquin, also used as a preservative has been associated with:- immune deficiency syndrome, leukaemia, blindness, skin, stomach, spleen, and liver cancer.

- Vitamin and minerals:
  - Choline Chloride
  - Calcium Panthenate
  - Thaimin Mononitrate
  - Riboflavin
  - Pyridoxine Hydrochloride
  - Folic Acid
  - Biotin
  - Menadione Dimethylprimidinol Bisulfite
  - Ascorbic Acid
  - Iron proteinate, ferrous carbonate and ferrous sulphate
  - Copper Oxide and copper proteinate
  - Copper Sulfate

This content has been tested at toxic levels (Martin, 2003).

- Food colouring:

Food colouring is added to this mix in order for it to be aesthetically pleasing to the consumer (i.e. the pet owner). This, and the way that the labels show meat as the upper most ingredient on the list (but is usually only between 4% & 30% of the content), convince us that this is a healthy meal of our beloved carnivorous pet.

- Visible vegetables – manufacturers have caught on to this trend and a few have added visible amounts of carrot and peas to their dog food. Unfortunately, carrots are mainly indigestible by dogs, although they make a great source of fibre and a tasty treat, and peas contain far too much sugar for them.

N.B.: There is no governing body for the regulation of the contents of pet food, it is all done by the individual manufacturer.

The Pet Food industry, unlike the human food industry are not obliged to list all the ingredients, nor are they obliged to list the contents in any sort of order. Therefore, they list the tiny "meat and animal derivative" content at the top to make you think that it is the most used ingredient.

Ingredient effects on digestion

The starch content and reduced protein content of dried and tinned foods, whilst increasing energy availability, inactivates lipase and pepsin by reducing the acidity of hydrochloric acid in the stomach. This has a negative effect on protein digestion (Brosey et al., 2000: Jin et al., 1994; Maskell & Johnson, 1993; Allen et al., 1981; Carpentier et al., 1977; Villareal et al., 1955) as well as on motility (Clemens & Stevens, 1980).

Dietary fibres, soy, corn and beet pulp further hinder digestion and impact the immune response (National Research Council, 2006; Silvio et al., 2000; Harmon et al., 1999; Field et al., 1999; Muir et al., 1996; Fernandez & Phillips, 1982; Burrows et al., 1982). This leads to dental disease (Baer & White, 1961; Auskaps et al., 1957) and consequently systemic diseases (Yudkin, 1969).

Manufactured pet foods are high in water soluble fibre. This is kept in the stomach for longer, slowing down stomach digestion (Fogle, 2002). They are also high in insoluble fibre, retaining water, speeding up movement through the intestines and bulking out faecal matter (Fogle, 2002); without which there would be diarrhoea (Strombeck, 1999).

This insoluble fibre may be fermenting or non-fermenting. Fermenting fibre is actively digested by bacteria in the large intestine. Slowing down transport and having a negative effect on the digestion of proteins (National Research Council, 2006).

Biologically appropriate food is high in fresh meat protein, and low in carbohydrates (Diez et al., 2002). Dogs actually have no requirement for carbohydrates in their diet (Baldwin et al., 2010; National Research Council, 1985).

Raw meat has 95% digestibility, a positive effect on stomach acid pH and absorption (National Research Council, 2006).

31

Effects of cooking

Cooking de-natures proteins (Fester Kratz, 2009: Pond, 2000), altering their physical and chemical structure by literally unfolding the genetic structure (Fester Kratz, 2009). Only folded polypeptides are functional. These control metabolism, transport, communication and basic cell function (Fester Kratz, 2009). Cooking proteins therefore as cooking proteins renders them inert, and all these basic functions will be adversely affected.

Cooking also impairs the storage stability of vitamins and minerals (Lugwigshafen *et al.,* 1984). Phospholipids found in the cell walls of plant and animal material - essential for the health of each living cell - are also broken down by heat. Phospholipids are needed in great quantities by the immune system (Pond, 2000).

This can go so far as to effect behaviour, with the nature of the amino acid Tryptophan being changed and the levels reduced by the cooking process. Tryptophan is the pre-cursor of (is needed to make) Seratonin, also known as 'the happy hormone', needed to produce a state of calm; low levels of Seratonin are associated with aggression.

Body condition effects of raw and cooked diets

Most cooked diets contain carbohydrates in the form of grains. These are often protein and fibre rich source of nutrition. However, the starch content has been known to increase weight gain.

Coat effects of Nutrition

A greying coat has been recognised as a "clear sign of zinc deficiency" (Burger & Rivers, 1989).

32

Course, dry hair is due to a deficiency of fat (Codner & Thatcher, 1990). This is often the first signs of a fatty acid deficiency, which can lead to visual impairment, polyneuropathy and reduced learning ability (Tinoco, 1979; Holman *et al.*, 1982; Neuringer *et al.*, 1988; Conner *et al.*, 1992; Uvay *et al.*, 1989). In addition, there may be renal and reproductive abnormalities, a decreased growth rate, a negative effect on the immune system, a weakening of cutaneous blood vessels, with an increased tendency to bruise, decreased wound healing, hypertrophy of sebaceous glands and an increase in water loss from the epidermis, along with other degenerative changes in organs and fragile cell membranes (Hansen *et al.* 1948 & 1954; Hansen & Weise, 1951; Weise *et al.* 1965 & 1966; Holman, 1971).

In order to grow a thick glossy coat, dogs need good quality protein and oils, with the nature of these being affected by the cooking process, there is also a likelihood of reduced gloss and increased dandruff.

Oral effects of raw and cooked diets

According to the British Association of Veterinary Dentistry (BAVD), 80% of dogs over the age of 3 have periodontal disease (see figure 4) (Milella, N.D.; Hamp *et al.*, 1984). This can constitue up to 40% of the workload of veterinary practices (Watkins, 2008). Susceptility to the disease increases with age (Cox & Lepine, 2009).

Bacteria found in tartar have been shown to produce an immunological response, (Warinner, 2012; Nonnemacher *et al.* 2002). Tartar in dogs has indeed been shown to impact the immune system (Lonsdale, 1995). It is logical then, that the larger the quantities of tarter, the greater the immune response. This in turn, could lead to further immune response of said animal to other pathogens, being reduced i.e. a sluggish immune system.

Periodontal diseases have been associated with degeneration of the hepatic, renal, circulatory and respiratory systems (DeBowes *et al.*, 1996; Pavlica *et al.*, 2008; Milella, 2012).

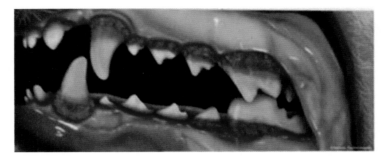

Figure 4 - 80% of 3yr old dogs have periodontal disease. (Milella, N.D.)

One of the first signs of periodontal disease is halitosis (Kortegaard *et al.* 2008; Zero, 2004; Rawlings & Culham, 1998; Benamghar *et al.*, 1982). This arises from the waste material of bacteria feeding on food debris attached to plaque, tartar and calculus, (Dogan *et al.* 2007) as well as a bacterial overgrowth of intestinal microflora (Barbara *et al.* 2005). This potentially leads to gum disease, as bacteria proliferate and begin to consume epithelial cells and blood.

In order to combat this problem, pet food manufactures are introducing polyphosphates into their diets, in order to reduce tartar (Cox & Lepine, 2002). Further, they have developed specialist chews, designed in shape and consistency to effectively "brush the teeth" of pets, as compared to manual and power brushing (Quigley & Hein, 1962). The aim is to reduce the need for dental surgery (Logan, 2006; Kortegaard *et al.* 2008).

A raw diet includes raw bones which, whilst they do have the potential to splinter and lodge in the gastro-intestinal tract, are much less likely to do so than cooked bones (Mash, 2011). They also give the animal the opportunity to clean their teeth via abrasion - a much easier option, with a quicker effect due to the chipping off of calculus and tartar, than the other recommended route of tooth-brushing (Rawlings & Culham 1998; Benamghar *et al.* 1982). It is also less costly than dental surgery (Cox & Lepine, 2009).

Faecal effects of raw and cooked diets

Commercial diets contain large quantities of non-digestible fibre, in order to increase the speed of peristalsis in the large intestine and prevent constipation. This makes for rather soft faecal matter.

Raw diets are generally high in bone content, not all of which is digested, making for harder faecal matter.

It could be argued that, whilst there is a risk of constipation on a raw diet, that conversely there is a risk of non-expressed anal glands with a cooked diet.

Scientific Research

The diagnosis of nutrient deficiencies is much more common than that of overdose (McNamara, 2006). Indication of deficiencies have been noted herein, with examples of:

- Crusty lesions of nares – indicating Vitamin A deficiency (Ackerman, 2008)
- Dry, scaly skin, brittle hair – indicating Biotin deficiency (Ackerman, 2008)
- Poor skin and coat condition – indicating Zinc deficiency (Ackerman, 2008)

A large differential was found in not only the way these animals were fed, but the constituent ingredients. When looked at in combination with details on how canine digestion functions, it shows that starchy foods (such as grains and potato) that are utilised in cooked diets to increase energy consumption, actually decrease the ability of the dog to digest protein, which is necessary for effective digestion in many areas of the gastro-intestinal tract. This negative effect on digestion, impacts nutritional absorption and therefore, cellular function. If each individual cell is malnourished, then so is the animal, because it has a further negative impact on immunity and thus health.

The consistency differential between cooked and raw foods has an effect on oral health, with soft cooked foods and crumbly dried foods having little to no effect on the removal of plaque. Bones, on the other hand, being highly abrasive, provide effective removal. Once more, the starch contained in cooked foods has an effect, as the energy feeds the bacteria present in plaque, starch is not able to be broken down in any way whilst in the oral cavity, due to the lack of amylase in canine saliva. Given that national statistics show that 80% of dogs over the age of 3 have periodontal disease (Millela, N.D.) and the number one diagnosis for dogs over the age of

3 in America is periodontal disease (Banfield Pet Hospital, 2012), it is evident that there are issues with oral health that relate highly to diet.

Other than a long term experiment by Francis Pottenger (1983), there is very little scientific research with regard to the differential between raw and cooked diets in pets. Pottengers' experiment showed a generational difference between cats fed a raw or cooked diet (see Table 1).

Cooked diet	Raw diet
Heterogeneous reproduction, with total sterility by the fourth generation	Reproductive ease
Physical degeneration, increasing with each generation	Optimal health
Smaller palates with over crowding and crossing of teeth	Wide palates with plenty of space for teeth
Bones became soft & pliable	Good bone structure and density
Vermin and parasites abounded	No parasites
Suffered from adverse personality changes	Gentleness
Suffered from hypothyroidism and most of the degenerative diseases encountered in human medicine	No disease

Table 1 - Generationally produced health of raw verses cooked diet in cats. (Pottenger, 1983)

An internet survey was launched in 2010, providing information on the life styles of dogs across three continents. The results speak for themselves.

- "56% of raw fed dogs had never or only once seen a vet (with median visits 1)

- All cooked fed dogs had seen a vet at least twice (with median visits 10)

- Feeding cooked food costs twice that of feeding raw food (average saving £240 per year)

- Veterinary costs and visits are 10 times higher for cooked fed dogs than raw fed dogs (average saving £1100)

- It costs 7 times less to have a healthier, happier dog

- Therefore the hypothesis *"What we put in our carnivores does make a difference as to health and longevity"* is valid"

To further this, a project was performed in 2012, comparing the visible health of dogs on cooked and raw diets (see Table 2). The results implied that raw-fed dogs are healthier.

	Cooked diet	Raw diet
Overweight	13%	0%
Underweight	23%	10%
Optimum Coat Gloss	32%	80%
Soft Coat	42%	70%
Dryness or grease to coat	55%	10%
Lack of dryness or grease to coat	45%	90%
Dandruff/Scale	52%	20%
Plaque Coverage	77%	0%
Halitosis	87%	0%

Table 2 – Results of "An Assessment of whether Cooked or Raw Diets Product Healthier Pet Dogs *(Canis lupus familiaris)* (Turner, 2012)

Case Study – Dawson

Dawson, a three year old Labrador retriever, presented with a number of issues:

- Underweight
- Losing weight
- Bald on chest & belly
- Allergies
- Skin issues
- Digestive issues
- Thin, pale coat
- Veterinary diagnosed as un-able to digest fats
- Diagnosed as Epileptic from 6 months of age
- Behavioural issues
- Last Fit was in March 2011.
- Weight as of 03/04/2012 – 25kg
- Previous Phenobarb levels registered at 25
- History of pica (eating plastic objects & pieces of rope).
- Due to have veterinary dentistry for calculus

On a prescription non-fat diet, 120mg of Epiphen (Phenobarbitone) twice a day for the epilepsy and 1mg of Prednicare (steroid) daily for his digestive, allergy and skin issues.

At the end of May 2012 his diet was altered to our 'complete' recipe (detailed on page 47), nothing else was changed.

Upon Veterinary advice his steroids were halved, by 16/07/2012 (6 weeks after the change in diet) they were stopped.

20/08/2012 Blood test: Phenobarb level 15 at 3 hour post pill, alt 76 – Phenobarb dose reduced to 30mg AM, 60 mg PM (90mg per day down from 120 mg per day).

- 100ml of Milkthistle per week added to diet

25/01/2013 Weight 28.5kg

30/01/2013 Blood tests: Phenobarb = 56 (65-194) L. Alt=44 AkP=62 Albumin=29.1 T.Bili=1.7

01/02/2013 Veterinary advice to further reduce Phenobarb levels to half initial level (30ml twice a day).

It is clear that the dietary change had an almost immediate effect on Dawson's digestive health, as well as his allergy and skin issues, reflected in his coming off the steroids permanently. He started putting on weight, but is not overweight; his coat has thickened up and re-grown on his chest; he now has beautifully white teeth without the need for veterinary dentistry. Further, his phenobarbitone prescription has been significantly reduced, however, his blood levels are up.

I am also informed that his behavioural issues stopped quite abruptly once this diet was changed.

Dawson is a much changed dog and his owners are converts for life.

What should your dog eat?

Whilst it must be accepted that, though many animals clean their food, they do not and cannot cook. The logical conclusion to that statement is rarely followed. Where humans' internal organs have changed over millennia to deal with our cooked diets, the physiology of animals has not, and even humans seem to fair better health wise, upon a switch to a diet high in raw foods.

Manufactured and pre-packed pet foods have only been available since the 1930's. Whilst animals produce more generations in 80 years than we do, it is not logical to assume that what has taken us millennia of evolution can be replicated in only 80 years with our pets. Animals fed manufactured, cooked pet food generally have breath, wind and waste issues, in comparison to their wild cousins. Yet, the general populous is not aware that these symptoms are a problem, as we have become habituated to them.

With a raw diet, pets no longer have breath problems, have white teeth, sleeker softer coats and have been shown to have improved health reducing veterinary visits by 85% (O'Driscoll, 2005).

Traditional veterinary surgeons do not generally promote raw feeding, claiming there are "dangers". They quote "salmonella", "bone splintering" and "increased worms". In fact, healthy raw meat feed animals have a higher immunity to salmonella and worms, and bones are much more likely to splinter if cooked than raw, especially using todays' food produce in which the meat is much younger and bones are therefore much more supple than previously available.

An experiment by Pottenger (1983) studying the difference between feeding raw and cooked food, provided results which would surprise many. He took two groups of cats and over a period of time, fed one group raw and the other group cooked food. The only difference in what was provided nutritionally was the cooking process. After several generations, the raw fed cats were significantly healthier than the original group and were living for longer. The cooked fed cats however, were very sick and producing mutations in their offspring. These diseases identified in the 'cooked fed' group, could not relate to a lack of Taurine (an essential amino acid required by cats), as the cooked food would have contained Taurine, if in smaller amounts than the raw diet.

There is a theory claiming that if there was such a huge "danger" to our animals eating fresh meat and bones, then their species would have died out millennia ago. However, we have only to look at the wolf - whose physiology is so perfect it has not needed to evolve for the last million years - to see that it is indeed what they have evolved to consume.

With regard to our carnivorous pets, whilst protein, grains, vegetables and oils would be found in a wild diet, the ratio found in tinned and dried food does not equate, with a much higher grain content than meat protein. Similarly, where would our herbivorous pets find cooked and dried grains, fruit and vegetables, not indigenous to their environment in the wild.

A lack or excess of one or many vitamins, minerals or essential fatty acids can lead to "major chronic diseases" (Food and Nutrition Board, 1989). If prolonged, this can be fatal (Roche, 1976). Malnourished animals are "likely to have a compromised immune system" (Agar, 2001). The escalation of illness in pets over the past decade implies some issue within the genetics and/or the daily lives of our pets. Just note how the average UK veterinary visit cost in 2000 was £62.01 (Bruce, 2001), while the average cost in 2009 rose to £254 (Petwise, 2009).

A raw diet is based on the premise that dogs are 99.8% wolf (Wayne, 1993) and should therefore eat a diet more akin to their ancestor. Books written on raw feeding with menu recommendations are often used as guides by pro-raw

44

feeders, dominated mostly by those of Ian Billinghurst (2001), Thomas Lonsdale (2001) (Australian Veterinary Surgeons) and Juliette de Baïracli Levy (1992).

Pet food manufacturers show clearly the science of their recipes and have shown that there are bacteria issues with raw food with regards to what goes and in and what comes out of the animal (Case *et al.,* 2011). Raw foods often have bacteria, which is also found upon elimination. However, as discussed earlier, a regular diet, high in the right kind of nutrients (i.e. fresh meat) means that the animal is unlikely to contract an infection from these bacteria.

Indeed, fresh meat & bone, fruit and vegetables, provide essential vitamins, minerals and lipids and add to the overall palatability of the diet.

Cottage cheese and live yogurt contain probiotic cultures, which aid digestion and replace the good bacteria in the gut, but preventing microbial colonisation, increasing absorption of the small intestine, and producing anti-E.coli factors inhibiting the growth of many bacteria, especially pathogenic gram-negative types (Ewing & Haresign, 1989). It is advised that live yogurt be given when on antibiotics (Lewis, Morris & Hand, 1988).

Egg and oils balance out the omega 3 and 6 content helping to promote healthy skin and coat (Billinghurst, 2001). Linseed Oil (high in Omega 3) must be cold pressed, due to the deleterious effect of n-hexane's combination with lysine (from the seed) in the chemical extraction process, as this forms 2,5-dimethylpyrrole (DeCaprio, Olajos & Weber, 1982) which is toxic (DeCaprio, Kinney & LoPachin, 2009), degenerating first the peripheral and then the central nervous system. Olive Oil is recommended to be extra virgin, as it is the least processed and therefore highest quality. That is to say, it is high in mono-unsaturates, omega 3 and vitamin E and good for lowering cholesterol (Billinghurst, 2001).

Garlic helps to boost the immune system by providing a hostile environment for parasites. It also helps maintain a healthy heart and circulatory system (Billinghurst, 2001).

A healthy raw diet does not contain grains. Whilst useful for fibre content in many diets, the combination of increased permeability of gastric mucosa and the reduction in pH by lactic acid given off by fermenting starches can lead to ulcers, and structural/functional damage to stratified squamous, cardiac and gastric epithelium. Grains in a natural canine diet would be minimal, i.e. the stomach contents of a field mouse. Many gastrointestinal diseases can be attributed to feeding the wrong diet (Stevens & Hume, 1995), leading to further issues with absorption and then nutrition or the lack thereof.

When should you start raw feeding?

Now. Don't delay, there is no need for a graduated switch-over. In fact, that rather defeats the object, with the starches and grains from his/her current diet having a negative effect on the digestion of a raw diet. On occasion, a stomach reaction has been noted, and a starve day may be necessary, but on the most part the dogs tuck in and thrive from day one.

Pay attention when first feeding bones, especially if your dog is not used to them. Ensure that they are chewed properly before digestion and don't be too surprised if eagerly inhaled chicken wings, etc. are brought back up for a second go.

Take into account that it will take a number of days to purge the system of the toxins previously taken in, and four to five weeks for the body to become completely used to the change.

It is recommended to take extensive photographs of body condition, coat and teeth prior to starting, in order for you to fully appreciate the differential after one month and six months of raw feeding.

How often should you feed?

The dogs' digestive system is set up to eat only once a day. Canine stomach acid is much stronger than that of a human, hence they can digest bone, etc. However, putting anything in it, reduces its' strength and only time with an empty stomach can bring it back to its full pH.

Feeding more than once a day, or providing the ability to graze, actually reduces the dogs ability to digest what it is being fed. With the gastro-intestinal tract being 80% of the immune system, multiple daily feeding has a negative effect on the immune system, increasing the likelihood of illness.

Therefore, feed your dog once a day (the occasional treat is fine) and a weekly starve day will help boost the digestive and immune system (N.B. not for epileptic/diabetic dogs). If in doubt, consult a holistic or raw feeding veterinarian.

Amounts

8 parts meaty bones

2 parts offal

2 parts fruit & vegetables

1 part supplements

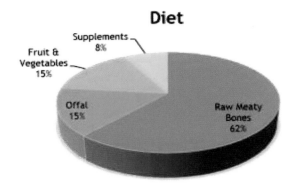

Diet

- Supplements 8%
- Fruit & Vegetables 15%
- Offal 15%
- Raw Meaty Bones 62%

As per the amounts to feed each individual animal, the answer is relevant to each metabolism. I am aware of a 27kg Labrador who eats 1lb/454g per day plus bones and a 35kg cross breed who eats up to 1kg per day. The best advice is to judge it by eye. Many dogs who have been converted to raw will eat vast quantities for quite some time as they are finally getting the right nutrients and are worried they won't again. Don't fear: they will calm down. I have yet to meet an overweight raw fed dog, as they become sated by their meals.

The risk of obesity is higher in cooked fed dogs, as they eat as much as possible in order to 'self medicate', attempting to ensure that they get all the vitamins and minerals necessary by eating more of the only option they have been given, and in the meantime becoming obese whilst nutritionally starving.

Details of recommendations for diet and treats are found in the recipes section.

Recipes

Diet:

Enough for a weeks' food for 1 medium to large dog.

2 kg Minced Chicken carcass

500 g Minced offal (ensure that the thyroid is not included)

100 g Apple

100 g Broccoli

100 g Carrots

100 g Red Peppers

75 g Mushrooms

25 g Blackberries

50 g Cottage Cheese

50 g Live Yogurt

1 Egg (including shell)

30 ml Cold Pressed Linseed Oil

30 ml Extra Virgin Olive Oil

65 g Alfalfa

30 ml Garlic

20 ml Echinacea

20 ml Seaweed

20 ml Nettle

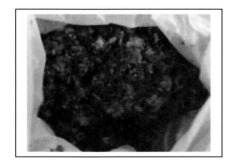

Serve with a variety of whole raw meaty bones.

Treats:

Please note the use of rice flour rather than wheat flour. Dogs do produce small amounts of Amylase (the enzyme necessary to digest starch) from their pancreas, and rice flour is digestible to them in small quantities. Also Scottish oats (used in K9 Cookies & Fish Cakes) are gluten free and therefore more appropriate than wheat flour. It is advised that these treats are given sparingly.

For regular treats use fruit or vegetables, my dogs prefer apples, carrots and bell peppers, occasionally small quantities of cheese, but one of the best for training is dehydrated liver or heart. To make these, cut the meat into strips, and leave on a low heat in the oven over night, or via use a dehydrator.

All biscuit-type treats require mixing, rolling, cutting out and baking. Oven time is dependent on thickness of biscuits and should be judged by you. I make them all into different shapes so that I can tell the difference and who prefers which.

Please note: as these contain no preservatives feed soon, or freeze for longer term keeping.

Pup Cakes

1lb/454 g Mince Offal

250g Rice Flour

100g grated carrot

75g Cottage Cheese

90 ml Extra Virgin Olive Oil

2 Eggs

30 ml Garlic

These can be made into celebratory cakes with a little imagination and some yogurt frosting.

K9 Cookies

150 g Oat Flour

100 g Rice Flour

150 g Minced Chicken

125 g Peanut Butter

100 g grated carrot

1 tsp Baking Soda

1 tsp Turmeric

Liver Snaps

1lb/454 g Mince Offal

250 g Rice Flour

90 ml Extra Virgin Olive Oil

30 ml Garlic

Push into a tray – bake, slice into 1cm lengths & re-bake.

Baa-Bix

250 g Rice Flour

150 g Minced Lamb

125 g Unsalted Butter

1 tsp Baking Soda

1 tsp Mint

Cluck-Bix

250 g Rice Flour

150 g Minced Chicken

125 g Unsalted Butter

1 tsp Baking Soda

1 tsp Rosemary

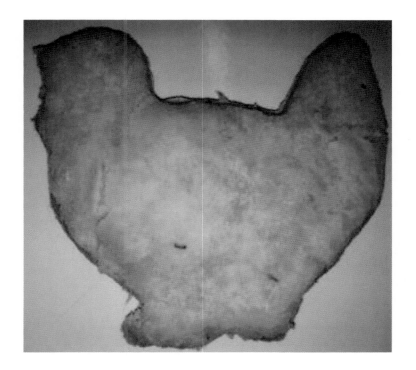

Dog Jellies:

Beef & broccoli

2 pints Beef Stock, made from boiling 125 g dried beef

100 g Broccoli

4 Tbs Gelatin

1 tsp Oregano

Chicken & Carrot

2 pints Chicken stock, made from boiling a chicken carcass

Remove carcass

150 g minced chicken

100 g carrots

4 tbs Gelatin

1 tsp Fenugreek

Once stock is ready and all meat, vegetables and herbs are in, add gelatin, ensure it melts and is well mixed, and allow to cool a little. Separate into treat sized containers and refrigerate until ready to serve. Should last around 4-5 days in the fridge.

Dog Stars

250 g Rice Flour

125 g Unsalted Butter

100 g Live Yogurt

1 large Banana

50 g Desiccated Coconut

50 g Powdered Almond

2 tbs Raw Honey

1 tsp Baking Soda

1 tsp Cinnamon

1 tsp Spirulina

Eek-Bix

250 g Rice Flour

150 g Cottage Cheese

125 g Unsalted Butter

1 tsp Baking Soda

1 tsp Poppy Seeds

Fish Cakes

250g Rice Flour

150g Fish

60 ml Cold Pressed Linseed Oil

1 Egg

1 tsp Parsley

Gobble-Bix

250 g Rice Flour

150 g Minced Turkey

125 g Unsalted Butter

1 tsp Baking Soda

½ handful chopped, dried Cranberries

1 tsp Cinnamon

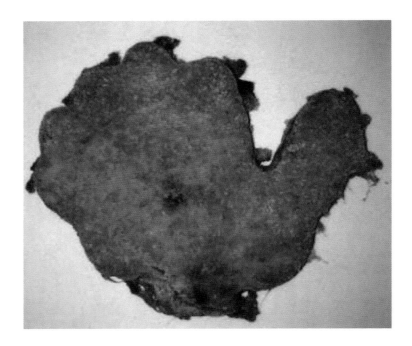

Grunt-Bix

250 g Rice Flour

150 g Minced Venison

125 g Unsalted Butter

1 tsp Baking Soda

½ handful chopped red currants

1 tsp Thyme

Hop-Bix

250 g Rice Flour

150 g Minced Rabbit

125 g Unsalted Butter

1 tsp Baking Soda

50 g Alfalfa

1 tsp Echinacea

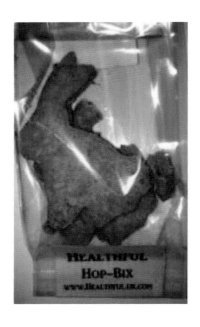

Moo-Bix

250 g Rice Flour

150 g Minced Beef

125 g Unsalted Butter

1 tsp Baking Soda

1 tsp Mustard Seeds

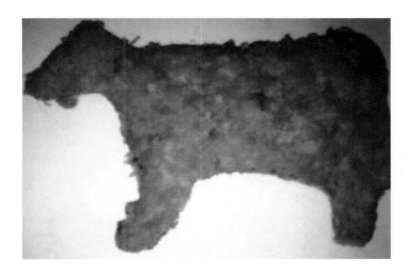

Oink-Bix

250 g Rice Flour

150 g Minced Pork

125 g Unsalted Butter

1 apple

1 tsp Baking Soda

1 tsp Sage

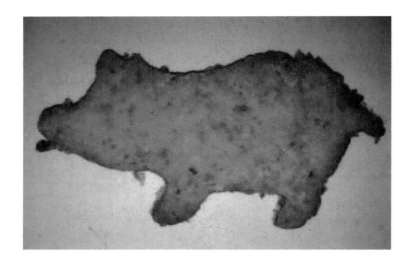

Pheasant Pie

250 g Rice Flour

150 g Minced Pheasant

125 g Unsalted Butter

1 tsp Baking Soda

1 tsp Oregano

Quack-Bix

250 g Rice Flour

150 g Minced Duck

125 g Unsalted Butter

1 tsp Baking Soda

1 Plum

1 tsp Ginger

Herbs and Spices

You have no doubt noticed the use of herbs and spices in my recipes. The following table provides the reasons that I use these:

Herb/Spice	Known to:
Alfalfa	Aid digestion cleanse kidneys
Basil	Aid digestion Anti-inflammatory Anti-oxidant Anti-viral Anti-microbial Anti-anxiety Expectorant
Cinnamon	Boost the immune system Boost circulation Anti-flatulent Anti-bacterial Anti-fungal Aids digestion Reduces blood sugar levels
Comfrey	Stimulate cell growth Anti-inflammatory Known as 'Knit-bone' due to it's propensity to speed the healing of broken bones
Dandelion	Anti-inflammatory Diuretic used to treat bile & liver problems
Echinacea	Boost the immune system

	Pain reliever Anti-inflammatory Anti-viral Anti-oxidant Improves coat condition
Fenugreek	Increase milk production Reduce glucose levels boost appetite
Garlic	Anti-oxidant Kill Worms Boost the immune system natural anti-biotic Lowers cholesterol Anti-cancer
Ginger	Aid digestion Reduces pain of osteoarthritis Lowers cholesterol Kill cancer cells
Milk Thistle	prevent & repair liver damage
Mint	Anti-flatulent Anti-Spasmodic Aids digestion Calmative Breath freshener
Mustard Seed	Anti-inflammatory Inhibits cancer growth Lowers blood pressure
Nettle	Diuretic Blood purifier Improves coat condition Pain relief for muscles, joints & arthritis
Oregano	Anti-Oxidant

	Anti-Bacterial Source of Vitamin K
Parsley	Diuretic Breath freshener
Rosemary	Anti-flatulent Improves coat condition
Sage	Anti-flatulent Improve appetite
Seaweed	Improves thyroid function Anti-viral Reduces worms Boost the immune system
Thyme	Antiseptic Anti-bacterial Anti-oxidant anti-spasmodic expectorant anti-cancer
Turmeric	Anti-inflammatory Natural anti-septic & Anti-biotic Liver detoxifier Aids fat metabolism Natural pain-killer Speeds up wound healing Used to treat: arthritis & rheumatoid arthritis inflammatory skin conditions Has been known to halt & even reverse the growth of certain cancers

FAQ's

Is there a right and a wrong oil?

Unfortunately, yes.

Chemically extracted oils pose a risk for any animal consuming them. The process leads to a chemical reaction between n-hexane and lysine in the original material. This forms 2,5-dimethylpyrrole (DeCaprio, Olajos & Weber, 1982) which is toxic (DeCaprio, Kinney & LoPachin, 2009), degenerating first the peripheral and then the central nervous system.

The other issue is whether the oils you are using are balanced as far as Omega's are concerned (3, 6 & 9), or if they have negative effect on absorption.

Cod liver oil for example, is so high in vitamin A, that it has a negative effect on the absorption of vitamin D. This has a domino effect on the absorption of calcium, and all that can lead to.

The answer is to only use cold-pressed oils, the two oils I recommend are, extra virgin olive oil and cold-pressed linseed oil, because of their balancing effects and the fact that they are not as immune-suppressing as fish oils.

Immunity & proteins

Any mammal's inherent immunity is reliant on many factors, 'The Compliment System' being one of the first and most important.

'Compliments' bind to anti-bodies, creating a catalyst to speed up an immune response and facilitate anti-bodies in targeting certain bacteria.

These 'compliments' are to do with proteins. Proteins are required for cellular repair, cellular membranes and as building blocks. It is therefore vital that every animal obtains the correct amount of amino acids from protein, in order to keep these cells and therefore the immune system, healthy.

Cooking de-natures proteins. (Pond, 2003)

Reasons not to feed corn or soy to your dog

Corn & Soy are made up of short-chain fatty acids that are known to inactivate lipase, hydrochloric acid & pepsin (Brosey *et al.* 2000). This inevitably has a negative effect on digestion, especially of proteins, and therefore the amino acids necessary for mood regulation.

Bloat

Deep chested breeds of dog are highly susceptible to bloat. This can lead to emergency surgery and the possibility of the dog not surviving.

So, how does your dog get bloat?

Bloat can occur due to a build up of gas trapped in the gastro-intestinal tract. This gas is created by micro-bacteria in the hind gut as a result of bacterial fermentation of starch.

Starch in the mammalian body is digested by amylase. However, dogs produce only very small quantities and therefore have no capacity to deal with the large amounts in commercial diets.

Small amounts of starch can be coped with in the canine diet, but large amounts of starch (such as found in dried and tinned foods, from grains, cereals, rice & potatoes) can and do lead to bloat and even death.

Pet food definitions: 100% Complete & Balanced

The definition of 100% Complete is that the food contains all the nutrients essential for life.

The definition of Balanced is that the food contains the minimum quantities necessary of all essential nutrients.

Therefore, a pet food can be labelled 100% Complete, but not be able to sustain life without the pet having to eat large quantities of it in order to obtain its minimum requirements. This leads the owner to believe that the pet enjoys the food and the pet towards obesity.

Patrick, J.S. (2006) *Deconstructing the Regulatory Façade: Why Confused Consumers Feed their Pets Ring Dings and Krispy Kremes.* [Internet] Available from: http://leda.law.harvard.edu/leda/data/784/Patrick06.html#fn77 (accessed 21/12/2011)

Lets' talk Shit!

Not the nicest part of pet ownership, but a necessary evil, it struck me how different it actually is between commercially-fed and raw-fed dogs.

That from commercially-fed dogs is large, generally soft if not runny, is particularly odourous, and is dark brown to black in colour.

However, that from raw-fed animals is small, hard, barely smells and is cream to white in colour.

This is quite important as the colouration of scat is obviously dependent on food, but also on dead blood cells.

Raw-fed animals generally only produce something black and possibly runny if fed too much liver or heart (both extremely high in blood).

However, commercially fed dogs pass dark-coloured scat all the time. Bearing in mind that the contents list assures us that there are not eating high quantities of blood in the commercial food, then it is more likely the dogs own dead blood being passed.

If this is the case, then commercially fed dogs are killing off their own blood cells at a phenomenal rate – much, much higher than raw-fed animals.

With so much energy having to go into new blood production, these dogs are much more likely to have a lowered immune system.

Scare tactics regarding bacteria in raw food

Pet food manufacturers educate veterinary surgeons to tell you that there are major risks involved in feeding raw food with regard to bacteria. Their scientists have identified bacteria in pet food and in the faeces of those pets fed it. However, they do not inform you that a dog on a fully raw, non-grain diet does not get affected by these bacteria.

Here is why:

Bile and pancreatic juice released into the duodenum are bactericidal for :

- E.coli
- Shigella
- Salmonella
- Klebsiella

and bacteriostatic for:

- Coagulase (+ & -)
- staphulocci
- pseudomonas

They also inhibit candida albicans.

National Research Council (2006) *Nutrient Requirements of Dogs and Cats.* Washington DC. The National Research Academic Press

E Numbers in pet food

The law now states that these have to be listed individually, so please feel free to check the bags/tins for yourself.

Antioxidants

- BHA aka **E320**

  Has been found to be tumour-producing when fed to rats. In human studies, it has been linked with urticaria, angioedema and asthma

- BHT aka **E321**

  Banned for use in food in Japan, Romania, Sweden, and Australia. The US has barred it from being used in infant foods. McDonalds have voluntarily eliminated it from their products.

- Propyl Gallate aka **E310**

  Banned from children's foods in the US because it is thought to cause the blood disorder methemoglobinemia

Colourants

- Iron Oxide aka **E172** (Rust)

  Banned in Germany

- Indigo Carmine aka **E132**

  Can cause skin sensitivity, a rash similar to nettle rash, itching, nausea, high blood pressure and breathing problems. One of the colours that the Hyperactive Children's Support Group recommends be eliminated from the diet of children. Banned in Norway.

- Tartrazine aka **E102**

  A trial on 76 children diagnosed as hyperactive, showed that tartrazine provoked abnormal behaviour patterns in 79% of them.

- Sunset Yellow aka **E110**

  Has been found to damage kidneys and adrenals when fed to laboratory rats. It has also been found to be carcinogenic when fed to animals

- Quinoline Yellow aka **E104**

  One of the colours that the Hyperactive Children's Support Group recommends be eliminated from the diet of children. Banned in Australia, Japan, Norway and the United States.

- Titanium Dioxide aka **E171**

  Found in most pet foods, it is a known carcinogen & is also the basis of the lovely white paint on your windows, ceilings & doors. Banned in Germany

- Carbon Black aka **E153**

  Banned as a food additive in the United States of America. Suspected as a carcinogenic agent.

If "you are what you eat", what does that make your dog?

In our current 'Nescafe Society', the Western World wants everything at the touch of a button and convenience food is a number one best seller. The link between these foods and obesity, diabetes and heart attacks has clearly been made and the government are attempting to educate the public about a healthy lifestyle of food and exercise in their "Change 4 Life" campaign (their bias being to help reduce the NHS costs incurred by a citizens' unhealthy lifestyle).

Thus the question becomes, who is there to do this for our pets?

The pet food companies? Their bias is sales!

The veterinarians? Most of their information comes direct from the pet food companies.

Who then? And what is in our conveniently packaged, well advertised, pet foods?

Pet food labelling does not come under the same laws as that of human food. Therefore, it can be somewhat vague. It may read: 'meat and animal derivatives, derivatives of vegetable origin, oils & minerals' – and little more. Some labels may be much more explicit, but appear to use a language all of their own e.g. 'poultry digest', 'gluten meal' etc. So how can the average pet owner discern the health qualities of each individual food?

Simply put, they can't.

Pet food manufacture swept the nation after World War I, when cavalry horses were surplus to requirements and therefore canned and sold as pet food. Nevertheless, when the horses ran out, so did the high meat content, and manufacturers found themselves needing a substitute.

Grains are cheap and have protein content and therefore made a logical replacement, in fact Britains' 'best selling' pet food is detailed as being 50% grain.

Scientists worked out which were the 'essential' vitamins and minerals necessary to keep a dog alive and these became the premise from which a product can be labelled "Complete". Minimum requirements of each of these, if met in the product, entitles it to be labelled "Balanced". This leaves the average pet owner not realising that the "Complete" pet food he or she is purchasing, may well be lacking or overdosing on certain nutrients, leaving a pet nutritionally imbalanced or even starving in certain areas. Symptoms of which are often attempts to self-medicate via stealing human food or some form of coprophagia, pica, soil eating, etc.

So, with this knowledge and a plethora of foods on the market, chose those which are both "complete" and "balanced" right?

If only it were that simple.

Not all of the pet food sold is Britain is made in Britain and therefore subject to British laws on ingredients or manufacturing process. Whilst the 'Pet Food Manufacturers Association' (PFMA) can assure us a certain quality of ingredients on 95% of British made foods, 'Made in Britain' is often a misnomer and actually only means that the item was packaged in Britain.

Outside of the UK "meat and animal derivatives" can mean euthanized pets, that much beloved dog, cat or horse, still containing barbiturates and even wearing their identity collars or chemical-infused flea collars. As these collars etc. are not 'intentionally added ingredients', the law does not require them to be listed.

OK, so that's what the 'meaty chunks' are?

Not necessarily.

Often those 'meaty chunks' are processed soy, high in protein and made to look like meat.

But the packet says "with Chicken"!

That means that the product in question contains a minimum of 4% chicken.

Armed with this information, now which way do you turn?

When it comes to dried, tinned or moist foods, it is tricky. A small number of manufacturers have a "closed recipe" on their product, which means that - whatever happens - the percentages of all ingredients do not change. These manufacturers may be happy to send you a list of ingredients so that you can be somewhat more reassured as to what you are feeding your pet.

OK, so what do you do?

Personally, I prepare my pets food myself. After studying canine nutrition and digestion for over a decade I feel able to get the balance right and I know 100% what my dogs are eating, how it affects their digestive tract, DNA and each individual cell in their bodies. Friends of mine that do the same and I often hear the words "that dog eats better than I do" and in all honesty, never a truer word were spoken.

References

Ackerman, N. (2008) *Companion Animal Nutrition.* Edinburgh. Elsevier.

Agar, S. (2001) *Small Animal Nutrition,* Butterworth Heinemann, London p. 77

Allen, S.E. Fahey, G.C. Corbin, J.E. Puch, J.L. & Frankin, R.A. (1981) Evaluation of By-product Feedstuffs as Dietary Ingredients for Dogs. *Journal of Animal Science.* **53**:1538-1544

Altman, P.L. & Dittmer, D.S. (1968) Digestion and Absorption. In: *Metabolism.* Bethesda, Md. Federation of American Societies for Experimental Biology.

Ashdown, R.R. (2008) Symposium on Canine Recto-Anal Disorders – 1: Clinical Anatomy. *Journal of Small Animal Practice.* **9**[7]:315-322

Auskaps, A. Grupta, O. & Shaw, J. (1957) Periodontal disease in the Rice Rat. III. Survey of Dietary Influences. *Journal of Nutrition.* **63**:325-343

Baer, P. & White, C. (1961) Studies on Periodontal Disease in the Mouse IV. The Effects of a High Protein, Low Carbohydrate Diet. *Journal of Periodontology.* **32**:328-330

Baldwin, K. Bartges, J. Buffinton, T. Freeman, L. Grawbow, M. Legred, J. & Ostwald, D. (2010) AAHA Nutritional Assessment Guidelines for Dogs and Cats. *Journal of the American Animal Hospital Association.* **46**:286-296

Banfield Pet Hospital (2012) *State of Pet Health 2012 Report.* [Online] Available from: http://www.stateofpethealth.com/pdf/State_of_Pet_Health_2012.pdf [accessed 07/07/2012]

Banta, C.A. Clemens, E.T. Krinsky, M.M. & Sheffy, B.E. (1979) Sites of Organic Acid Production and Patterns of Digestive Movement in the Gastrointestinal Tract of Dogs. *J. Nutr.* **109**:1592-1600

Barbara, G. Stanghellini, V. Brandi, G. Cremon, C. Di Nardo, G. De Giorgio, R. & Corinaldesi, R. (2005) Interactions Between Commensal Bacteria and Gut Sensorimotor Function in Health and Disease. *The American Journal of Gastroenterology.* **100**:2560-2568

Benamghar, L. Penaud, J. Kaminsky, P. Abt, F. & Martin, J. (1982) Comparison of Gingival Index and Sulcus Bleeding Index as Indicators of Periodontal Status. *Bulletin of World Health Organisation.* **60**[1]:147-151

Billinghurst, I. (2001) *The Barf Diet,* Warrigal Publishing, New South Wales, Australia p. 17, 29-46

Bradshaw, J. (2006) The Evolutionary Basis for the Feeding Behavior of Domestic Dogs (Canis familiaris) and Cats (Felis catus) *Journal of Nutrition.* **136**:1927-1937

British Veterinary Journal (1876) Advert British Veterinary Journal **4**

Brosey, B.P. Hill, R.C. & Scott, K.C. (2000) Gastrointestinal Volatile Fatty Acid Concentrations and pH in Cats. *American Journal of Veterinary Research.* **61**:359-361

Bruce, K. (2001) *Dog Owners Voice Concern Over High Vet Fees*, [Online] K9 Online, K9 Media Solutions Ltd, Notts, from: http://www.pressbox.co.uk/detailed/International/Dog_Owners_Voice_Concern_Over_High_Vet_Fees_1064.html (accessed 07/04/2010)

Budiansky, S. (1992) *The Covenant of the Wild – Why Animals Choose Domestication.* Pheonix, London (p.22-25, 72-86)

Burger, I.H. & Rivers, J.P.W. (1989) *Waltham Symposium 7 Nutrition of the Dog and Cat.* Cambridge University Press. Cambridge p. 14

Burns, J. (2009) *Domestic Dog Origins Challenged*, BBC News, from: http://news.bbc.co.uk/1/hi/sci/tech/8182371.stm (accessed 06/03/2010)

Burrows, C.F. Kronfeld, D.S. Banta, C.A. & Merritt, A.M. (1982) Effects of Fibre on Digestibility and Transit Time in Dogs. *Journal of Nutrition.* **112**:1726-1732

Carpentier, Y. Woussen-Cokre, M.C. & de Graef, J. (1977) Gastric Secretions from Denervated Pouches and Serum Gastrin Levels After Meals of Different Sizes of Meat Concentration in Dogs. *Gasteroenterol Clinical Biology.* **1**:29-27

Carriere, F. Moreau, M. Raphel, V. Largier, R. Berricourt, C. Junien, J. & Verger, R. (1991) Purification and Biochemical Characterizaion of Dog Gastric Lipase. *Eur. J. Biochem.* **202**:75-83

Case, L. P., Hayek, M.G., Daristotle, L. & Raasch, M.F. (2011) *Canine & Feline Nutrition*, Moseby Inc, Missouri p. 170

Clemens, E.T. & Stevens, C.E. (1980) A Comparison of Gastrointestinal Transit Time in Ten Species of Mammals. *Journal of Agricultural Science.* **94**:735

Clutton-Brock, J. (1999) *A National History of Domesticated Mammals*, Cambridge University Press. Cambridge, (Inside Cover, p 25-128, 190-191)

Codner, E.C. & Thatcher, C.D. (1990) The Role of Nutrition in the Management of Dermatoses. *Semin. Vet. Med. Surg. (Sm. Animal)* **5**:167-177

Conner, W.E. Nuringer, M. & Reisback. S. (1992) Essential Fatty Acids: The Importance of n-3 Fatty Acids in the Retina and Brain. *Nutr. Rev.* **50**:2129

Cornell University (N.D.) *Study of the Molecular Basis of Tame and Aggressive Behavior in the Silver Fox Model*: from: http://cbsu.tc.cornell.edu/ccgr/behaviour/index.html (Accessed 06/03/2010)

Cox, E.R. & Lepine, A.J. (2002) 2793 Use of Polyphosphates in Canine Diets to Control Tartar. Seq #257 – Nutritional Factors and Dental Health. *IADR/AADR/CADR 80th General Session* (March 6-9, 2002) San Diego, California

Cox, E.R, & Lepine, A.J. (2009) Influences on Dental Health in the Field Dog. *P&G Pet Care Publications*. **4**[1]:51-58

Coyne, J.A. & Orr, M.A. (2004) *Speciation*, Sinam Assoc. Inc. Maryland. p. 83-124

Darwin, C. (1859) *The Origin of Species*. Murray, London

De Baracli Levy, J. (1992) *The Complete Herbal Handbook for the Dog and Cat*. Faber and Faber, London

DeBowes, L. Mosier, D. & Logan, E. (1996) Association of Periodontal Disease and Histologic Lesions in Multiple Organs from 45 Dogs. *Journal of Veterinary Dentistry*. **13**[2]:57-60

DeCaprio, A.P. Olajos, E.J. & Weber, P. (1982) Convalent Binding of neurotoxic n-hexane metabolite: Conversion of Primary Amines to Substitued Pyrrole Adducts by 2,5-hexandedione. *Toxicology and Applied Pharmacology*. **65**[30]:440-450

DeCaprio, A.P. Kinney, E.A. & LoPachin, R.M. (2009) Comparative Convalent Protein Binding of 2,5-hexanedione and 3-acetyle-2,5-hexandione in the rat. *Journal of Toxicology and Environmental Health* Part A 72[14]:261-9

Defra (2011) *Pet Food Manufacturers*. [Online] Defra, London. Available from: http://animalhealth.defra.gov.uk/managing-disease/animalbyproducts/food-and-feed-businesses/pet-food-manufacture.htm#5 (Accessed 25/04/2012)

Diez, M. Nguyen, P. Jeusette, I. Devois, C. Istasse, L. & Biourge, V. (2002) Weight Loss in Obese Dogs: Evaluation of a High-Protein, Low-Carbohydrate Diet. *Journal of Nutrition.* **132**:1685-1687

Dobzhansky, T. Ayala, F. J. Stebbins, G. L. & Valentine, J. W. (1977) *Evolution*, W. H. Freeman & Co., San Francisco. p.96

Dogan, E. Okumus, Z. & Yanmaz, L. (2007) Periodontal Diseases in Pet Animals. *Veterinary Research.* **1**[1]:17-22

Erasmus, U. (1993) *Fats that Heal – Fats that Kill.* Canada. Alive Books.

Ewing, W. & Haresign, W. (1989) *The Guide to Probitotics in the United Kingdom.* Chalcome Publications, Bucks. p. 1-5

Fernandex, R. & Phillips, S.F. (1982) Components of Fibre Impair upon Iron Absorption in the Dog. *American Journal of Clinical Nutrition.* **35**:107-112

Fester Kratz. R. (2009) *Molecular and Cell Biology for Dummies.* New Jersey. Wiley Publishing Inc.

Food and Nutrition Board (1989) *Recommended Dietary Allowances*, National Academies Press, Washington D.C. p1-9

Fogle, B. (2002) *Caring for your Dog.* Dorling Kindersley Ltd. London

Field, C.J. McBurney, M.I. Massimino, S. Hayek, M.G. & Sunvold, G.D. (1999) The Fermentable Fibre Content of the Diet Alters the Function and Composition of Canine Gut Associated Lymphoid Tissue. *Veterinary Immunology and Immunopathology.* **72**:325-341

Goody, P.C. (1997) *Dog Anatomy.* J.A. Allen, London

Gordon, P.H. (2001) Anorectal Anatomy and Physiology. *Gastroenterology Clinics of North America.* **30**[1]:1-13

Griffith, C. (2012) The Best Dog Diet Ever by Caroline Griffith. Love, Woof & Wonder Publishing. UK

Hamp, S.E. Olsson, S.E. Farso-Madsen, K. Vilands, P & Fornell, J. (1984) A Macroscopic and Radiological Investigation of Dental Diseases in the Dog. *Veterinary Radiology.* **25**:86-92

Hansen, A.E. Weise, H.F. & Beck. O. (1948) Susceptibility to Infection Manifested by Dogs on a Low Fat Diet. *Fed. Proc.* **7**:289

Hansen, A.E. & Weise, H.F. (1951) Fat in the Diet in Relation to Nutrition of the Dog. I Characteristic Appearene and Gross Changes of Animals fed Diets with and without Fat. *Tex. Rep. Biol. Med.* **9**:491-515

86

Hansen, A.E. Sinclair, J.G. & Weise, H.F. (1954) Sequence of Histologic changes in Skin of Dogs in Relation to Dietary Fat. *J. Nutr.* **52**:541-554

Harmon, D.L. Walker, J.A. Silvio, J.M. Jamikorm, A.M. & Gross, K.L. (1999) Nutrient Digestibility in Dogs Fed Fibre-containing Diets. *Veterinary Clinical Nutrition.* **6**:6-8

Hemmer, H., (1990) *Domestication – the decline of environmental appreciation*, Cambridge University Press, Cambridge p. 35-80

Holman, R.T. (1971) Essential Fatty Acid Deficiency. *Prog. Chem. Fats Lipids.* **9**:275-348

Holman, R.T. Johnson, S.B. & Hatch, T.F. (1982) A case of Human Linolenic Acid Deficiency involving Neurological Abnormalities. *Am. J. Clin. Nutr.* **35**:617-623

Jin, H.O. Lee, K.Y. Chang, T.M. Chey, W.Y. & Dubois, A. (1994) Physiological role of Cholecystokinin on Gastric Emptying and Acid Output in Dogs. *Digestive Diseases and Sciences.* **39**:2306-2314

Kamath, P.S. Hoepfner, M.T. & Phillips, S.F. (1987) Short-chain Fatty Acids Stimulate Motility of the Canine Ileum. *American Journal of Physiology.* 4:G427-G433

Kelly, N. & Wills, J. (1996) *Manual of Companion Animal Nutrition and Feeding*, BSAVA, Gloucester p. 254

Ken-L-Ration (1932) Advertisement

Kortegaard, H. Eriksen, T. & Baelum, V. (2008) Periodontal Disease in Research Beagle Dogs – An Epidemiological Study. *Journal of Small Animal Practice.* **49**:610-616

Lewis, L.D. Morris, M.L. & Hand, M.S. (1988) *Guide to Dietary Management of Small Animals.* Mark Morris Associates, Topeka, Kansas. p. 6

Logan, E. (2006) Dietary Influences on Periodontal Health in Dogs and Cats. *Veterinary Clinic of North American Small Animal Practice.* **36**[6]:1385-1401

Lonsdale, T. (1995) *Raw Meaty Bones: Promote Health*, Rivetco, New South Wales
Lugwigshafen, N. A. Bonn, G. B. Elmshorn, D. D. Hess.Olend, W. K. Cuxhaven, K. K. Grenzach, H. L. (1984) *Vitamins in Animal Nutrition,* AWT, Bonn p.42

Martin, A.N. (2003) Food Pets Die For. New Sage Press, Oregon

Mash, H. (2011) *The Holistic Dog.* The Crowood Press Ltd. Marlborough

Maskell, I.E. & Johnson, V. (1993) Digestion and Absorption p.25-44 In: The Waltham Book of Companion Animal Nutrition. Burger, I. Ed Oxford, Pergamon Press

McNamara, J.P. (2006) *Principles of Companion Animal Nutrition.* New Jersey. Pearson Prentice Hall.

Mech, L.D. (1970) *The Wolf – The Ecology and Behaviour of an Endangered Species.* University of Minnesota Press, Minneapolis p. 168-192

Mech, L.D. & Boitani, L. (2003) *Wolves: Behavior, Ecology and Conservation.* Chicago. University of Chicago Press.

Milella, L. (N.D.) *Understanding the Need for Dental Treatment in Dogs.* Educational Resources for Veterinarians. British Veterinary Dental Association

Milella, L. (2012) Prophylactic Dental Care in Cats. *Veterinary Nursing Journal.* **27**:14-16

Morey, D. F. (2006) *Burying Key Evidence: the Social Bond Between Dogs and People*, Journal of Archaeological Science, 33[2]:158-175

Muir, H.E. Murray, S.M. Fahey, G.C. Merchen, N.R. & Reinhart, G.A. (1996) Nutrient Digestion by Ileal Cannulated Dogs as Affected by Dietary Fibres with Various Fermentation Characteristics. *Journal of American Science.* **74**:1641-1648

National Research Council (1985) *Nutrient Requirements of Dogs.* Washington D.C. National Academic Press

National Research Council (2006) *Nutrient Requirements of Dogs and Cats.* Washington DC. The National Academic Press

Neuringer, M. Anderson, G.J. & Conner, W.E. (1988) The Essentiality of the n-3 Fatty Acids for the Development and Function of the Retina and Brain. *Am. Rev. Nutr.* **8**:517-541

Nonnenmacher, C. Flores-de-Jacoby, L. Dalpke, A. Zimmerman, S. Mutters, R. & Hegg, K. (2002) 0767 DNA from Periodontopathogenic Bacteria Induces Mouse and Human Cells to Produce Cytokines. *IADR/AADR/CADR 80th General Session* (March 6-9, 2002) San Diego, California

O'Driscoll, C. (2005) *Shock to the System.* Abbeywood Publishing (Vaccines) Ltd. London

Ostrander, E.A. & Wayne, R.K. (2005) The Canine Genome. *Genome Research.* **15**:1706-1716

Pavlica, Z. Petelin, M. Juntes, P. Erzen, S. Crossley, D. & Skaleric, U. (2008) Periodontal Disease Burden and Pathological Changes in Organs of Dogs. *Journal of Veterinary Dentistry.* **25**[3]:97-105

Pedigree Pet Foods, (1993) *Product Information*, Waltham, Leicester

Pet Food Institute (2010) *How Dry Pet Food Is Made.* [Online] Washington DC: Pet Food Institute. Available from: http://www.petfoodinstitute.org/Index.cfm?Page=DryPetFood (Accessed 25/04/2012)

Petwise, (2009) *Why Insure your Pet?,* Petwise Health Insurance, from: http://www.petwise-insurance.co.uk/pages/whyinsure.asp (accessed 07/04/2010)

PFMA (2011) *Has the Market Changed Over the Years?* (Internet) Available from: http://www.pfma.org.uk/statistics/index.cfm?id=133&cat_id=58 Pet Food Manufacturers Association, London (accessed 06/10/2011)

Pond, C. M. (2000) *The Fats of Life,* Cambridge University Press, Cambridge p. 5-26

Pottenger, F. (1983) *Pottenger's Cats – A Study in Nutrition*, Price-Pottenger Foundation Inc, California

Purina (N.D.) *Spillers Foods 1851-1900.* [Online] Available from: http://www.purina.co.uk/apps/OurHistory/OurHistory.aspx?NRMODE=Publish ed&NRNODEGUID=%7BC25C061A-D25F-4A26-820A-616900CC6EE7%7D&NRORIGINALURL=%2FHome%2FAbout%2BPurina%2FOur%2BCompany%2FOur%2BHistory.htm&NRCACHEHINT=Guest [accessed 06/10/2011]

Quigley, G.A. & Hein, J.W. (1962) Comparative Cleaning Efficacy of Manual & Power Brushing. *Journal of American Dental Association.* **65**: 26-29

Rawlings, J. & Culham, N. (1998) Halitosis in Dogs and the Effect of Periodontal Therapy. *Journal of Nutrition.* **128**:2715-2716

89

Riddle, M. (1987) *Dogs Through History*, Denlinger, Virginia p. 8-59

Roberts, M. (1996) *The Man Who Listens to Horses.* Arrow, London

Roche (1976) *Vitamin Compendium*, F. Hoffmann-La Roche & Co. Ltd, Basle, Switzerland p. 7

Rolfe, V.E. Adams, C.A. Butterwick, R.F. & Batt, R.M. (2002) Relationships between Fecal Consistency and Colonic Microstructure and Absorptive Function in Dogs with and without Nonspecific Dietary Sensitivity. *American Journal of Veterinary Research.* **63**[4]:617-622

Savolainen, P. Arvestad, L. & Lundeberg, J. (2000) mtDNA Tandem Repeats in Domestic Dogs and Wolves: Mutation Mechanism Studied by Analysis of the Sequence of Imperfect Repeats. *Molecular Biology.* **17**[4]:474-488

Scheppach, W. (1994) Effects of Short Chain Fatty Acids on Gut Morphology and Function. *Gut.* **35**:S35-S38

Serpell, J. (1995) *The Domestic Dog: Its Evolution, Behaviour and Interaction with People.* Cambridge University Press, Cambridge. p. 9-10

Silvio, J. Harmon, D.L. Gross, K.L. & McLeod, K.R. (2000) Influence of Fiber Fermentability on Nutrient Digestion in the Dog. *Nutrition.* **16**[4]:289-295

Skelton, P. (1993) Evolution – A Biological and Palaeontologial Approach. The Open University, Milton Keynes. p.917-994

Stevens, C.E. & Hume, I.D. (1995) *Comparative Physiology of the Vertebrate Digestive System*. Cambridge University Press, Cambridge. p. 183, 224-228

Strombeck, D.R. (1999) *Home-prepared Dog and Cat Diets.* Iowa. Iowa State University Press.

Tinoco, J. (1979) Dietary Requirments and Functions of α-Linolenic Acid in Animals. *Prog. Lipid. Res.* **21**:1-46

Townend, L. (2009) *Animals in the Womb: Dogs*, Channel 4, London
Turner, H.B. (2012) An Assessment of whether Cooked or Raw Diets Produce Healthier Pet Dogs *(Canis lupis familiaris).* Unpublished.

Uvay, R. Peirano, P. & Hoffman, D.R. (1989) Essential Fatty Acid Metabolism and Requirements during Development. *Sem. Perinatol.* **13**:118-130

Villareal, R. Ganong, W.F. & Gray, S.J. (1955) Effet of Adrenocorticotrophic Hormone upon the Gastric Secretion of Hydrochloric Acid, Pepsin and Electrolytes in Dogs. *American Journal of Physiology.* **183**:485-494

Warinner, C. (2012) *Tracking Ancient Diseases using ... plaque.* [Online] TED. Available from: http://www.ted.com/talks/christina_warinner_tracking_ancient_diseases_usin g_plaque.html (Accessed 24/04/2012)

Watkins, J.D. (2008) Letter Submitted to the Veterinary Record. June 7 2008

Wayne, R. K. (1993) Molecular Evolution of the Dog Family. *Trends in Genetics.* **9**[I6]:218-224 1/6/93, Elsevier Ltd, Oxford

Wayne, R. & Vila, C. (2001) *The Genetics of the Dog; Phylogeny and Origin of the Domestic Dog.* Wallingford: CAB. International. p. 1-13

Weise, H.F. Bennet, M.J. Coon, E. & Yamanaka, W. (1965) Lipid Metabolism of Puppies as Affected by Kind and Amount of Fat and of Dietary Carbohydrate. *J. Nutr.* **86**:271-280

Weise, H.F. Yamanaka, W. Coon. E. & Barber, S. (1966) Skin Lipids of Puppies as Affected by Kind and Amount of Fat and of Dietary Carbohydrate. *J. Nutr.* **89**:113-122

Wolfcountry.net (N.D.) Wolf Origins. From: http://www.wolfcountry.net/information/WolfOrigins.html (Accesse 08/03/2010)

Yudkin, J. (1969) Dental Decay is Preventable: Why not prevented? *Br. Dent. J.* **127**[9]:425-429

Zero, D. (2004) Sugars – The Arch Criminal? *Journal of Caries Research.* **28**:277-285

Useful Links:

British Association of Homoeopathic Veterinary Surgeons	www.bahvs.com
American Holistic Veterinary Medical Association	www.ahvma.org
Raw Food Vets	www.rawfoodvets.com
Dogucation Events	www.facebook.com/DogucationEvents
Canine Health Concern	www.canine-health-concern.org.uk
Price Pottenger Nutrition Foundation	www.ppnf.org
Healthful	www.healthful.uk.com